REMARKABLE PEOPLE

Edward Kennedy

by Steve Goldsworthy

BOOK CODE

T30176

AV² by Weigl brings you media enhanced books that support active learning.

AV² provides enriched content that supplements and complements this book. Weigl's AV² books strive to create inspired learning and engage young minds for a total learning experience.

Go to **www.av2books.com**, and enter this book's unique code. You will have access to video, audio, web links, quizzes, a slide show, and activities.

Audio
Listen to sections of the book read aloud.

Video
Watch informative video clips.

Web Link
Find research sites and play interactive games.

Try This!
Complete activities and hands-on experiments.

Due to the dynamic nature of the Internet, some of the URLs and activities provided as part of AV² by Weigl may have changed or ceased to exist. AV² by Weigl accepts no responsibility for any such changes. All media enhanced books are regularly monitored to update addresses and sites in a timely manner. Contact AV² by Weigl at 1-866-649-3445 or av2books@weigl.com with any questions, comments, or feedback.

Published by AV² by Weigl
350 5th Avenue, 59th Floor
New York, NY 10118
www.av2books.com   www.weigl.com

Library of Congress Cataloging-in-Publication Data

Goldsworthy, Steve.
 Edward Kennedy / Steve Goldsworthy.
   p. cm. -- (Remarkable people)
 Includes index.
 ISBN 978-1-61690-169-1 (hardcover : alk. paper) -- ISBN 978-1-61690-170-7 (softcover : alk. paper) -- ISBN 978-1-61690-171-4 (e-book)
 1. Kennedy, Edward M. (Edward Moore), 1932-2009--Juvenile literature. 2. Legislators--United States--Biography--Juvenile literature. 3. United States. Congress. Senate--Biography--Juvenile literature. I. Title.
 E840.8.K35G65 2010
 973.92092--dc22
 [B]
                                2010006162

Printed in the United States of America in North Mankato, Minnesota
1 2 3 4 5 6 7 8 9 0 14 13 12 11 10

052010
WEP264000

Editor: Heather Kissock
Design: Terry Paulhus

Photograph Credits
Weigl acknowledges Getty Images as the primary image supplier for this title.

Every reasonable effort has been made to trace ownership and to obtain permission to reprint copyright material. The publishers would be pleased to have any errors or omissions brought to their attention so that they may be corrected in subsequent printings.

Contents

Who Is Edward Kennedy?

Edward "Ted" Kennedy was a United States **senator** from Massachusetts and a member of one of America's best-known political families, the Kennedys. His brother, John, was elected president of the United States in 1960. Another brother, Robert, was elected to the Senate in 1964. Both brothers' lives ended tragically. John F. Kennedy was **assassinated** three years into his presidency. Robert was assassinated while **campaigning** for the **Democratic Party** presidential **nomination** in 1968.

"We have never lost our belief that we are all called to a better country and a newer world."

Like his brothers, Ted chose politics as a career. He was first elected to the Senate in 1962. He served for 46 years, one of the longest terms in history. Ted was known as the "Lion of the Senate" because of his long service and strong influence.

Ted ran for president in 1980 but lost his party's nomination to returning president Jimmy Carter. Ted continued to serve as a senator and a member of the Democratic Party until his death on August 25, 2009.

Growing Up

Edward Moore Kennedy was born February 22, 1932, in Boston, Massachusetts, to wealthy financier and politician Joseph P. Kennedy and his wife, Rose Fitzgerald. Ted had three older brothers, Joseph, John, and Robert, and five sisters, Eunice, Patricia, Jean, Kathleen, and Rosemary. Ted was the youngest of the Kennedy children.

Joseph Kennedy built his wealth by working in banking, shipbuilding, and movie distribution. In the 1930s, he began a political career by accepting chairperson positions on government **commissions**. In 1938, President Franklin D. Roosevelt named Joseph the United States **ambassador** to Great Britain.

Joseph's work meant that the family moved around quite a bit. By the age of 11, Ted had attended 10 different schools. He was known as a good, but not remarkable, student. Ted was much better at sports, especially football.

■ As the youngest of the Kennedy children, Ted was often compared to his older brothers.

Get to Know Massachusetts

HORSE
Morgan Horse

FLAG

BIRD
Black-capped
Chickadee

The official name of the state is the Commonwealth of Massachusetts. Its nickname is the "Bay State" due to its location by the ocean.

Boston is the state's capital city. This is where the Boston Tea Party took place. The Boston Tea Party was a key event leading up to the American Revolutionary War.

Boston founded the first library in the United States in 1653.

Alexander Graham Bell invented the telephone in Boston in 1876.

Massachusetts has a state muffin, the corn muffin, and a state cookie, the chocolate chip cookie.

Think about it!

Massachusetts was the home of many revolutionary ideas that shaped the United States. Ted Kennedy and his brothers had many ideas that became laws. These laws offered the people of the United States more freedom and liberty. What ideas do you have for making the world a better place? They could include an invention, a new law, or just a better way of doing something.

Practice Makes Perfect

Ted followed the Kennedy tradition and entered Harvard University in 1950. He was suspended when he was caught cheating on a test. In an effort to change his ways, Ted enlisted in the U.S. Army before re-entering Harvard in 1953.

Ted's father had always put a strong emphasis on education and encouraged Ted to try his best. Ted listened to his father and improved his grades, but it was in football that he excelled. He quickly became one of the most valuable players on his team. A football scout noticed Ted's skill. He asked Ted if he wanted to play football professionally. Ted declined, explaining that he wanted to pursue a political career.

■ Ted Kennedy was offered a tryout for the Green Bay Packers football team.

After graduating from Harvard with a degree in history and government, Ted went on to earn a degree in law from the University of Virginia. While taking his law degree, Ted helped his brother John campaign for Senate re-election in 1958. Ted's friendly attitude and ability to connect with people contributed to his brother's win.

Established in 1636, Harvard University is the oldest school for higher learning in the United States.

Key Events

In 1960, Ted's brother John ran for president of the United States. Before he could run, however, John had to persuade members of the National Democratic Party, known as delegates, to vote for him. John turned to Ted to run his campaign in the western states. With his charming personality and fun attitude, Ted won over many delegates. He rode horses in rodeos, attempted ski jumping, and earned his pilot's license so he could fly across the west to promote his brother. Ted's efforts helped his brother win the Democratic presidential nomination as well as the presidential election. John F. Kennedy became the 35th president of the United States.

When he became president, John had to leave his job as a senator. Ted was offered his brother's Senate position, but he was not able to accept it. Ted was 28 years old at the time, and senators must be at least 30 years of age. Instead, Ted became an assistant district attorney. His job was to help **prosecute** criminals. Ted ran for senator in the next election, and, on November 7, 1962, he was elected senator for the state of Massachusetts.

■ At 43 years of age, John F. Kennedy was the youngest person ever elected president of the United States.

Thoughts from Ted

Throughout his political career, Ted had a reputation for giving great speeches. He used the power of his words to inspire U.S. citizens and his fellow senators.

Ted discusses his views on the future of the United States.

"For all my years in public life, I have believed that America must sail toward the shores of liberty and justice for all. There is no end to that journey, only the next great voyage. We know the future will outlast all of us, but I believe that all of us will live on in the future we make."

Ted states his opinion on resolving conflict.

"It's better to send in the Peace Corps than the Marine Corps."

After Hurricane Katrina hit New Orleans, Ted comforts the country.

"This disaster reminds us that we are all part of the American family and we have a responsibility to help members of that family when they are in need."

After losing a leadership race for the presidency, Ted has this to say.

"The work goes on, the cause endures, the hope still lives, and the dream shall never die."

Ted gives a speech at his brother Robert's funeral.

"(Bobby was) a good and decent man, who saw wrong and tried to right it, saw suffering and tried to heal it, saw war and tried to stop it."

Ted states his views on democracy.

"Integrity is the lifeblood of democracy. Deceit is a poison in its veins."

What Is a Senator?

A senator is a member of the United States Senate. The United States Senate is the upper house of the **bicameral** United States **Congress**. Two senators represent each state. They serve staggered terms of six years each. Senators are elected by the people of their state. Each senator must be at least 30 years old, a U.S. citizen for the past nine years, and live in the state he or she represents.

Senators have a range of responsibilities. First, they represent the interests of their home state to the U.S. government. As part of the Senate, senators confirm the appointments of high-ranking U.S. officials, including Supreme Court judges, ambassadors, and **Cabinet** members. They also work together to **ratify treaties** and carry out **impeachment** cases. Most importantly, the Senate works closely with the House of Representatives. This is the lower house of Congress. Together, they create and pass the laws of the United States.

■ The Senate Chamber, where senators meet, is located in the United States Capitol.

Senators 101

John F. Kennedy (1917–1963)

John F. Kennedy began his political career in the U.S. House of Representatives. There, he represented Massachusetts from 1947 to 1953. He was then elected to Congress as a senator, and served from 1953 to 1960. As a senator, John was known to work for better **social welfare** and labor programs. He continued this focus into his presidency.

Robert Kennedy (1925–1968)

Robert Kennedy was elected to the Senate in November 1964, after serving as Attorney General since 1961. He became critical of the Vietnam War and encouraged laws that supported human rights and social welfare. Robert was campaigning to become a candidate for the presidency when he was assassinated in 1968.

Hillary Rodham Clinton (1947–)

Hillary began her political career as a student at Yale Law School. She spent her summers working for government committees in Washington. In 1975, Hillary married Bill Clinton and helped him become president of the United States. After leaving the White House, Hillary served as a senator for New York State from 2001 to 2009. In 2008, she ran for the presidential nomination for the Democratic Party. However, she lost to Barack Obama. In 2008, President Obama appointed Hillary the 67th United States **secretary of state**.

Barack Obama (1961–)

Barack Obama graduated from Harvard Law School and became a **civil rights** attorney in Chicago. He also taught law at the University of Chicago Law School. In 2004, Barack was elected as U.S. senator for the state of Illinois. He served in the position until 2008, when he was elected president of the United States. Barack is the first African American ever to be elected president.

Politicians

Politicians are people who run federal, state, and local governments. Their job is to make and pass laws for the people of the area or country they represent. Politicians are elected by the people they serve. To make sure the voice of the people is being represented, the United States holds elections every two to four years.

Influences

Ted Kennedy came from a large family. As American ambassador to Great Britain, Ted's father, Joseph, was often away from home. While Joseph was away on business trips, Ted's mother, Rose, stayed home raising all nine children alone.

Rose believed it was important to have a solid education. She often conducted pop quizzes around the dinner table with the children. They discussed science, literature, art, and history. The family often debated politics. These discussions motivated Ted to become an effective speaker. He would research a subject he wanted to talk about so that he would be prepared for family discussions. These conversations also encouraged his curiosity. Ted learned to ask questions to find out more about a topic or issue.

■ The Kennedy children spent much of their time sailing. The family took weekly sailing trips. Ted and his brothers and sisters often entered sailing races.

One of Ted's greatest influences growing up was his grandfather. John "Honey Fitz" Fitzgerald was a former mayor of Boston and a U.S. Representative. Ted loved his grandfather's charm and way with words. He adopted that attitude in his own political career.

THE KENNEDY FAMILY

Ted Kennedy married Virginia Joan Bennett on November 29, 1958, at St. Joseph's Church, in Bronxville, New York. Ted met Joan a year earlier while at law school. She was a student who had worked as a model. Ted and Joan had three children together, Kara Anne, Edward Jr., and Patrick. Ted's marriage to Joan ended in divorce in 1982. Ted remarried in 1992. His second wife was Victoria Reggie, a Washington, D.C. lawyer.

■ Ted's son Edward Jr. lost a leg to bone cancer. Edward Jr.'s illness influenced Ted's fight for better health care in the United States.

Overcoming Obstacles

Ted's life was one of highs and lows. Having two brothers assassinated impacted him greatly. However, he did not let their deaths stop him from pursuing a political career. Ted continued to fight for the issues he believed in. His long career in the Senate is proof of his determination to serve his country.

A few months after John's death, Ted almost died. He was on a plane that crashed in Westfield, Massachusetts. Ted survived the crash, but was hospitalized for a long time. He used the time to observe the health care system and form ideas about improving it. Ted took many of these ideas to the Senate and campaigned for health care reform. Changes have taken place because of Ted's efforts.

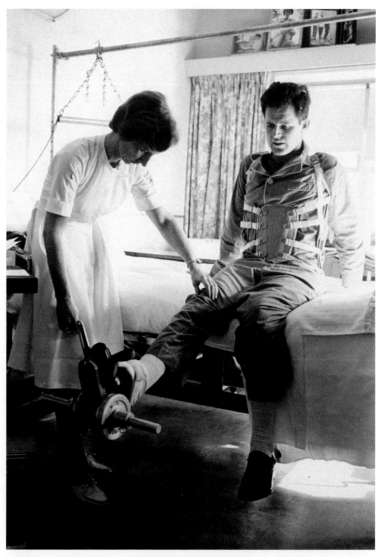

■ On June 19, 1964, Ted was in a plane crash that left him with a broken back, a collapsed lung, and two broken ribs. It was months before Ted could walk again.

In 1969, Ted's political career was deeply impacted when he was involved in a car accident. The accident resulted in the death of a passenger in Ted's car. Ted accepted responsibility for the accident. He then focused on his job as senator and continued to serve his country.

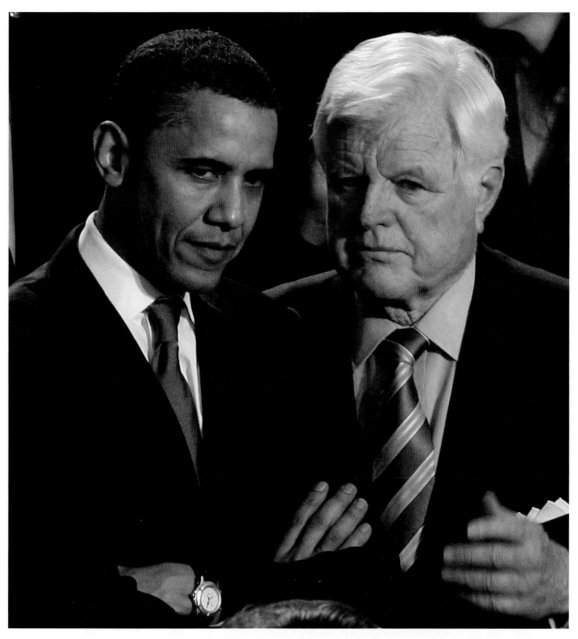

■ On January 28, 2008, Ted Kennedy declared his support for Barack Obama as the Democratic Party leader for the 2009 presidential election. Ted's support helped Obama win the nomination and, later, the presidency.

Achievements and Successes

In his long and productive career, Ted Kennedy did much for the country. During his time in office, Ted and his staff had more than 300 bills made into law. One of the causes he worked hardest to improve was health care. As a senator, Ted had a major influence on the country's health care system. He became chairman of the Senate subcommittee on health care. There, he helped create and pass the National Cancer Act of 1971. This act put $100 million into funding cancer research.

Ted was the driving force behind passing the Americans with Disabilities Act of 1990. This act bans **discrimination** on the basis of a person's disabilities. Ted had a personal reason for getting this act passed. His older sister Rosemary was mentally disabled, and his oldest son lost a leg due to an illness.

■ Senator Ted Kennedy announced he would run for leader of the Democratic Party in 1980.

As Chairman of the Senate Health, Education, Labor, and Pensions Committee, Ted worked to achieve affordable health care for all U.S. citizens. He also campaigned for laws concerning health insurance, **AIDS** care, and children's health care.

Ted also had an impact on international issues. He helped pass the Immigration and Nationality Act of 1965. This act helped more people become U.S. citizens. Ted worked with leaders of foreign countries to stop the building of nuclear weapons. He fought for human rights, social justice, and democracy throughout the world.

THE EDWARD M. KENNEDY INSTITUTE

The Edward M. Kennedy Institute for the United States Senate was created in Ted Kennedy's memory. It seeks to educate people about the role and importance of the Senate. Located on the campus of the University of Massachusetts in Boston, the institute is beside the John F. Kennedy Presidential Library. The institute focuses on improving education in the nation and inspiring a new generation of citizens and lawmakers. People can learn about the Senate by participating in mock Senate sessions and debate. They can also review important moments in Senate history. Most of the institute's resources are made up of reports Ted wrote and audio and videotapes of his many speeches.

Write a Biography

A person's life story can be the subject of a book. This kind of book is called a biography. Biographies describe the lives of remarkable people, such as those who have achieved great success or have done important things to help others. These people may be alive today, or they may have lived many years ago. Reading a biography can help you learn more about a remarkable person.

At school, you might be asked to write a biography. First, decide whom you want to write about. You can choose a senator, such as Ted Kennedy, or any other person you find interesting. Then, find out if your library has any books about this person. Learn as much as you can about him or her. Write down the key events in the person's life. What was this person's childhood like? What has he or she accomplished? What are his or her goals? What makes this person special or unusual?

A concept web is a useful research tool. Read the questions in the following concept web. Answer the questions in your notebook. Your answers will help you write your biography.

Edward Kennedy

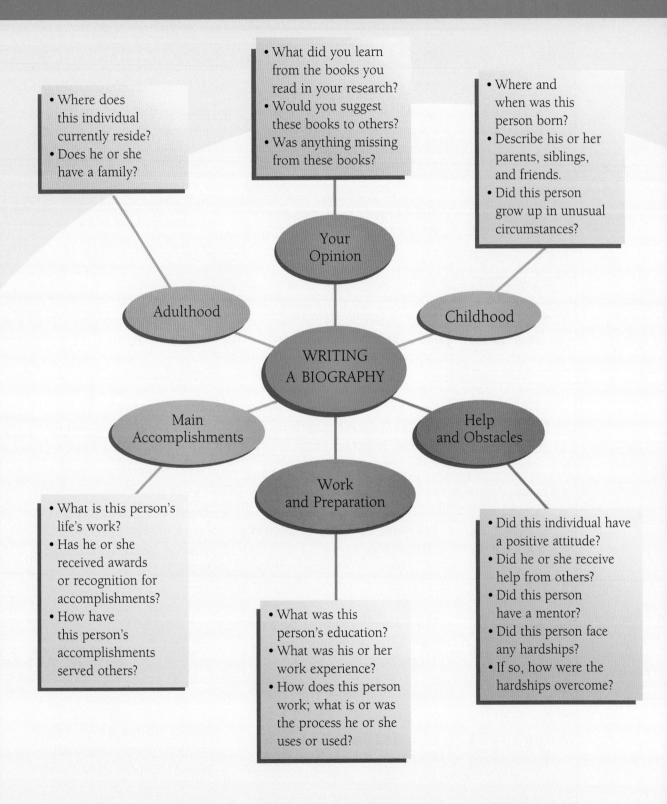

- Where does this individual currently reside?
- Does he or she have a family?

- What did you learn from the books you read in your research?
- Would you suggest these books to others?
- Was anything missing from these books?

- Where and when was this person born?
- Describe his or her parents, siblings, and friends.
- Did this person grow up in unusual circumstances?

Your Opinion

Adulthood

Childhood

WRITING A BIOGRAPHY

Main Accomplishments

Help and Obstacles

Work and Preparation

- What is this person's life's work?
- Has he or she received awards or recognition for accomplishments?
- How have this person's accomplishments served others?

- What was this person's education?
- What was his or her work experience?
- How does this person work; what is or was the process he or she uses or used?

- Did this individual have a positive attitude?
- Did he or she receive help from others?
- Did this person have a mentor?
- Did this person face any hardships?
- If so, how were the hardships overcome?

Timeline

YEAR	EDWARD KENNEDY	WORLD EVENTS
1932	Edward Kennedy is born on February 22.	Franklin D. Roosevelt is elected president of the United States.
1956	Ted Kennedy graduates from Harvard with a degree in history.	Dwight D. Eisenhower is elected president of the United States for a second term.
1962	Ted Kennedy is elected to the Senate.	Uganda gains independence from Great Britain.
1963	President John F. Kennedy, Ted's brother, is assassinated.	Martin Luther King Jr. delivers his "I have a dream" speech during the March on Washington.
1964	Ted Kennedy is almost killed in a plane crash.	The United States passes its Civil Rights Act. The act outlaws racial discrimination in public places.
1980	Ted Kennedy loses the Democratic presidential nomination to Jimmy Carter.	Ronald Reagan is elected president of the United States.
2009	Edward Kennedy dies of cancer.	Barack Obama is sworn in as the first African American president of the United States.

Words to Know

AIDS: Acquired Immune Deficiency Syndrome; a disease that destroys the body's ability to fight illness

ambassador: a government official sent to live in another country as a representative

assassinated: killed by a surprise or secret attack

bicameral: having two houses or chambers

Cabinet: a board that advises the president

campaigning: implementing a plan to win an election

civil rights: the rights belonging to a citizen of a country

commissions: groups of people given specific responsibilities and tasks to perform

Congress: the law-making body of the United States

democracy: a form of government in which the power lies with the people

Democratic Party: one of the two major political parties in the United States

discrimination: the unfair treatment of a person because of his or her race, gender, age, or physical or mental condition

impeachment: the process by which a government official is accused of improper behavior

nomination: deciding which politician will represent a party in the race for president

prosecute: to carry out legal action against someone in a court of law

ratify: to approve after a lengthy process

secretary of state: a high-ranking politician who handles foreign affairs for the government

senator: an elected politician who helps make decisions about the laws of the country

social welfare: well-being of a society

treaties: formal agreements between countries

Index

Log on to www.av2books.com

AV² by Weigl brings you media enhanced books that support active learning. Go to **www.av2books.com**, and enter the special code inside the front cover of this book. You will gain access to enriched and enhanced content that supplements and complements this book. Content includes video, audio, web links, quizzes, a slide show, and activities.

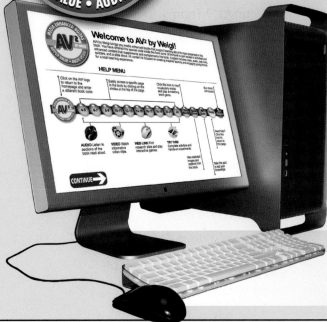

Audio
Listen to sections of the book read aloud.

Video
Watch informative video clips.

Web Link
Find research sites and play interactive games.

Try This!
Complete activities and hands-on experiments.

WHAT'S ONLINE?

Try This! Complete activities and hands-on experiments.	**Web Link** Find research sites and play interactive games.	**Video** Watch informative video clips.	**EXTRA FEATURES**
Pages 6-7 Complete an activity about your childhood.	**Pages 8-9** Learn more about Edward Kennedy's life.	**Pages 4-5** Watch a video about Edward Kennedy.	**Audio** Hear introductory audio at the top of every page
Pages 10-11 Try this activity about key events.	**Pages 14-15** Find out more about the people who influenced Edward Kennedy.	**Pages 12-13** Check out a video about Edward Kennedy.	**Key Words** Study vocabulary, and play a matching word game.
Pages 16-17 Complete an activity about overcoming obstacles.	**Pages 18-19** Learn more about Edward Kennedy's achievements.		**Slide Show** View images and captions, and try a writing activity.
Pages 20-21 Write a biography.	**Pages 20-21** Check out this site about Edward Kennedy.		**AV² Quiz** Take this quiz to test your knowledge
Page 22 Try this timeline activity.			